Forgotten Heroes
of the
American Revolution

HENRY KNOX

Washington's Artilleryman

FORGOTTEN HEROES
OF THE AMERICAN REVOLUTION

Forgotten Heroes of the American Revolution

HENRY KNOX

Washington's Artilleryman

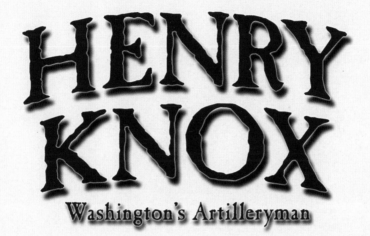

Richard M. Strum

OTTN PUBLISHING
STOCKTON, NJ

DEDICATION: For my friends and colleagues at Fort Ticonderoga.

Frontispiece: American soldiers guide a train of oxen that is transporting cannons from Fort Ticonderoga to Boston. Henry Knox's success in this difficult endeavor helped the Patriots win an early victory and made him one of George Washington's most trusted officers.

OTTN Publishing
16 Risler Street
Stockton, NJ 08859
www.ottnpublishing.com

First printing

1 3 5 7 9 8 6 4 2

Library of Congress Cataloging-in-Publication Data

Strum, Richard M.
  Henry Knox : Washington's artilleryman / Richard M. Strum.
      p. cm. — (Forgotten heroes of the American Revolution)
  Includes bibliographical references and index.
  ISBN-13: 978-1-59556-013-1
  ISBN-10: 1-59556-013-0
  ISBN-13: 978-1-59556-018-6 (pbk.)
  ISBN-10: 1-59556-018-1 (pbk.)
  1. Knox, Henry, 1750-1806—Juvenile literature. 2. Generals—United
States—Biography—Juvenile literature. 3. United States. Continental
Army—Biography—Juvenile literature. 4. United States—History—Revolution,
1775-1783—Campaigns—Juvenile literature. 5. Washington, George, 1732-
1799—Friends and associates—Juvenile literature. 6. Cabinet officers—United
States—Biography—Juvenile literature. 7. United States—Politics and
government—1783-1809—Juvenile literature. I. Title.
  E207.K74S77 2007
  973.3092—dc22
  [B]
                                    2006023083

Publisher's Note: All quotations in this book come from original sources, and contain the spelling and grammatical inconsistencies of the original text.

TABLE OF CONTENTS

Why Henry Knox Should Be Remembered

"The Council of Officers are unanimously of opinion, That the Command of the Artillery should no longer continue in Col: Gridley, and knowing of no person better qualified to supply his place, or whose Appointment will give more general satisfaction, have taken the liberty of recommending Henry Knox, Esqr to the consideration of the Congress."

—George Washington, letter to Continental Congress, November 8, 1775

"Genl Knox, who has deservedly acquired the Character of One of the most valuable Officers in the Service, and who, combating almost innumerable difficulties in the department he fills, has placed the Artillery upon a footing, that does him the greatest Honor."

—George Washington, letter to Continental Congress, May 31, 1777

"It is with peculiar Pleasure . . . that the Commander in Chief can inform General Knox and the Officers of Artillery that the Enemy have done them the Justice to acknowledge that no Artillery could be better served than ours."

—George Washington, general orders for June 29, 1778, following the Battle of Monmouth

"[Knox] was particularly remarkable for the attention he paid to the artillery service, a branch of military science for which he always [showed] a predilection. . . . The energetic spirit of the young man, and the handsome manner in which he executed a task, abounding with what some would have considered impossibilities, attracted the especial notice of Washington, and Knox, in consequence, was rewarded with the command of this very artillery. . . . He owed his advancement, in part also, to his superior knowledge of the department, there being, at that period, few persons in America competent for the office."

— Charles J. Peterson, in *The Military Heroes of the Revolution with a Narrative of the War of Independence* (1848)

"Knox was one of those providential characters which spring up in emergencies, as if they were formed by and for the occasion."

—Washington Irving, in *Life of George Washington* (1859)

"One of the most impressive developments in the Continental army was the creation of the artillery arm. Not even in existence at the beginning of the war, this branch of the service grew to a point where big guns became the decisive factor in the Yorktown campaign. . . . Henry Knox was the person primarily responsible for this amazing expansion."

—North Callahan, in *George Washington's Generals and Opponents: Their Exploits and Leadership*, edited by George Athan Billias (1994)

"It was the daring and determination of Knox himself that had counted above all. The twenty-five-year-old Boston bookseller had proven himself a leader of remarkable ability, a man not only of enterprising ideas, but with the staying power to carry them out."

—David McCullough, in *1776* (2005)

George Washington stands atop Dorchester Heights with one of the cannon batteries that forced the British to evacuate Boston in March 1776. The Patriot victory—Washington's first during the Revolution—was made possible by 25-year-old Henry Knox.

1

DORCHESTER HEIGHTS

General William Howe, commander of the British troops in North America, was livid. It was the morning of March 5, 1776, and somehow, overnight, the *rebels* had built what appeared to be a strong fort atop Dorchester Heights. From this high position, the Americans could fire down on British troops in the city of Boston and threaten British ships in the city's harbor. "The rebels have done more in one night than my whole army would have done in a month!" he roared.

WASHINGTON'S PLAN

The fortification of Dorchester Heights was part of General George Washington's plan to force the British out of

Boston. He had ordered his men to bring captured cannons from Fort Ticonderoga to Cambridge through the winter snows, so they could be placed on Dorchester Heights. But secrecy was essential to Washington's plan. If the British army learned what the Americans were doing, the **redcoats** could easily storm the Heights and prevent the cannons from being placed there.

On the night of March 2, the American *artillery* opened fire on the British in Boston as a distraction. Washington hoped to convince General Howe and other British officers that the Continental Army planned to attack Boston on the north side. General Washington moved troops and supplies to support an attack on the north, making sure the British could see his preparations. The British were fooled.

On the night of March 4, the American artillery again opened fire with a prolonged bombardment. Under the cover of the bombardment, General John Thomas, with 2,000 men and 400 oxen, dragged cannons to the top of Dorchester Heights. Unable to build real earthworks without the British hearing the men at work with entrenching tools, General Thomas used *fascines* (bundles of sticks tied together) made earlier to build quick *redoubts*. When dawn arrived on March 5, these temporary redoubts, with cannons pointed down at the city and out on the British navy in the harbor, appeared strong

Because the Continental Army had to work quickly, their initial fortifications on Dorchester Heights consisted of fascines like the ones pictured here. Continental soldiers had prepared these bundles of sticks beforehand, and on the night of March 4, 1776, a division commanded by General John Thomas (inset) carried them up the hill.

to the British below. The ***Continentals*** continued to reinforce the redoubts, which grew stronger and more difficult to attack every day.

A CONTINENTAL VICTORY

The cannons put the British position in the city of Boston and the British fleet in Boston Harbor at risk. As General

British soldiers board small boats during the evacuation of Boston, March 17, 1776.

Howe was soon to learn, the British in Boston and on the naval vessels in the harbor could not elevate their guns high enough to return fire. Howe and Rear Admiral Molyneaux Shuldham had two options—attack the fortifications to remove the rebel cannons, or withdraw from Boston after nearly 11 months of occupation.

The British tried to dislodge the rebels from their positions on Dorchester Heights, but a violent wind and rain storm caused the attack to fail. After nearly two weeks of indecision, General Howe acknowledged the strength of the rebel positions and ordered an evacuation of Boston by British troops. On March 17, 1776, more than 13,000 British troops, 60 British vessels, and nearly 1,100 loyal colonists left Boston by boat, headed to Halifax, Nova Scotia.

The evacuation of Boston was a great victory for the young Continental Army and a humiliating defeat for General William Howe, commander in chief of British forces in North America. One man, a 25-year-old colonel in the Continental Army, deserved most of the credit for forcing the British out of Boston, his hometown. That man was Henry Knox.

—FAST FACT—

March 17 remains an important holiday in Boston. While many celebrate the day as St. Patrick's Day, the holiday is still known as Evacuation Day, commemorating the anniversary of the British withdrawal from Boston in 1776. The city celebrates with a grand parade, dinners, essay contests, and scores of other activities. In recognition of the historic connection between Fort Ticonderoga and Boston, the Fort Ticonderoga Fife & Drum Corps participates in the festivities each year.

2

EARLY LIFE

Henry Knox was born in Boston on July 25, 1750. He was the 7th of 10 sons of William Knox and Mary Campbell. His father owned a wharf on Boston's waterfront and was a shipmaster.

Until the age of nine, young Henry attended the Boston Latin Grammar School. His formal education came to an early end in 1759, however. William Knox, deep in debt after the failure of his business, fled to the West Indies, leaving his large family in financial straits. Henry had to leave school to help support his mother and brothers.

He landed a job at Messrs. Wharton and Bowe, book-sellers. There he thrived. He took advantage of the lulls

This view of Henry Knox's hometown of Boston, showing men working on a wharf, appeared in a German publication during the 1770s.

between customers to read voraciously. Though he couldn't attend school, he was able to continue expanding his knowledge through reading. Henry read Greek and Latin classics in translation, and he learned to read French. But he especially liked to read books on military history and engineering sciences—two subjects that would serve him well in coming years.

As a young teen, Henry Knox joined a *militia* company of artillery known as "The Train." The company drilled in Boston under the command of a British officer. During the winter of 1766, Henry had the opportunity to train with a British regular artillery unit when the unit's departure for Quebec was delayed by bad weather. This experience gave him valuable skills he would use in the future.

HENRY KNOX, BOOKSELLER

Only days after his 21st birthday, Henry Knox opened his own bookstore. Though still just a young man, he had 12 years of experience in the business, and he managed to compete successfully with Boston's seven other bookstores until the outbreak of the American Revolution. In addition to books, Knox's London Book-Store sold a variety of items, including snuff, flutes, patent medicines, telescopes, wallpaper, and even cricket bats.

The London Book-Store became a popular gathering place for both British officers and **_Loyalist_** ladies. But it was also frequented by men who would play a role in the fight for American independence, including Paul Revere, John Adams, and especially Nathanael Greene. Knox and Greene

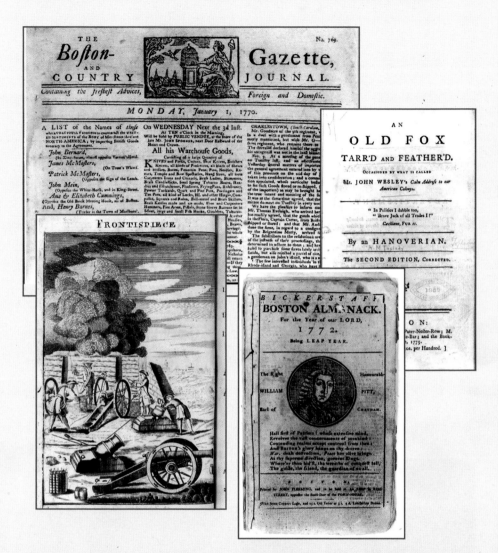

Pictured are a variety of publications that might have been sold in Knox's London Book-Store. They include (clockwise from top left): a Boston newspaper from January 1770; a reprint of a political pamphlet; a copy of *Bickerstaff's Boston Almanack* from 1772; and an illustration from a book on artillery, showing cannons and mortars at a fortress. Visitors to Knox's bookstore included John Adams (opposite page, right) and Nathanael Greene (opposite page, left).

began a lifelong friendship by discussing books on military history and engineering during Greene's many visits to Boston from Rhode Island.

By 1771, when he opened the London Book-Store, Henry Knox stood over six feet tall. He was stocky—a few would call him husky—but he was not yet the fat, genial man who stares out from the famous Gilbert Stuart portrait. Customers found the up-and-coming young merchant with the penetrating gray eyes amiable, intelligent, and charming.

LOVE AND MARRIAGE

One frequent customer was a young lady who, like Henry Knox, was very fond of books. Lucy Flucker was the daughter of Thomas Flucker, the royal secretary for the province of Massachusetts Bay. She and Henry Knox fell in love. Lucy's Loyalist parents objected to her involvement

Although Thomas Flucker (shown here) had a powerful position as royal secretary for Massachusetts, he was unable to prevent his daughter Lucy from marrying Henry Knox in 1774.

with the strongly patriotic Knox, but the courtship continued. By March of 1774, the young couple discussed marriage.

In a letter to Lucy, Henry Knox asked hopefully if she had mentioned marriage to her parents yet. "What news?" he inquired. "Have you spoken to your father, or he to you upon the subject? What appearance has this (to us) grand affair at your house at present?" Thomas Flucker prohibited a match between the two as long as Knox held on to rebellious beliefs. But the couple married anyway, on June 16, 1774. Lucy was 18 years old, and her husband 23.

Thomas Flucker tried to sway his new son-in-law to the Loyalist side. Lucy's only brother was a lieutenant in the British army. Through his government connections, Lucy's father arranged for Henry Knox to be offered a commission in the British army. Knox politely declined the offer.

GROWING TENSIONS

As Lucy and Henry Knox established their new household, the political situation between Great Britain and its colonies deteriorated. Knox's involvement in the militia placed him on the front lines of this growing dispute in Massachusetts Bay.

Back in March 1770, Henry Knox had tried to intervene at the Boston Customs House before the British guards—after being pelted with snowballs, sticks, and stones—

Bostonians dressed as Indians throw crates of tea into Boston Harbor, December 16, 1773. In response to the Boston Tea Party, the British government closed the port in 1774—a move that affected merchants like Knox.

opened fire on a mob in a deadly incident that **Patriots** called the Boston Massacre. Knox knew Captain Preston, the commander of the guard, perhaps as a customer at his bookstore.

Later, in December 1773, a group of Patriots unhappy with the British tax on tea boarded merchant ships in Boston Harbor and threw boxes of tea overboard. This event became known as the Boston Tea Party.

Following the Boston Tea Party, Parliament passed a number of punitive measures, including the Boston Port Bill. That bill ordered the closing of Boston Harbor until

the colonists paid for the destroyed tea. On June 1, 1774—
just two weeks before Henry Knox and Lucy Flucker were
married—the British navy closed the Port of Boston. For
Henry Knox, this was not a mere inconvenience; it threatened his livelihood. Knox purchased almost everything he
sold in his bookstore from London. In May, his agent in
London wrote that "as the Boston Port Bill takes place the
beginning of June am at a loss to know in what way to for-
ward" his latest order. Knox's solution was to have all ship-
ments sent to Salem, Massachusetts, and then arrange for
them to be shipped overland to Boston from there.

As tensions continued to grow in early 1775, General
Thomas Gage, now also the royal governor of Massachusetts, kept a close eye on noted Patriots. Henry Knox was
among those not allowed to leave Boston without permission. Within a month after the battles at Lexington and
Concord in April 1775, Henry and Lucy Knox gathered a
few belongings and slipped out of Boston, leaving their
home and business behind. Their lives would never be the
same. The coming war that would separate the colonies
from Great Britain also separated Lucy, forever, from her
Loyalist family.

GUNS FOR GENERAL WASHINGTON

Shortly after the fighting broke out between the rebel colonists and the king's troops at Lexington and Concord, Massachusetts, in April 1775, Henry Knox reported to the rebel commander to offer his services. Before George Washington's appointment as commander of the Continental forces in mid-June, General Artemas Ward, a veteran of the French and Indian War, commanded rebel forces outside of Boston. Knox's knowledge of artillery and fortifications earned him a position as a volunteer in charge of constructing rebel earthworks surrounding British-held Boston.

Before beginning his service for the Continental Army, Knox took his wife to Worcester to stay with friends out of harm's way. For much of the next eight years, the Knoxes would be apart, staying in touch by writing lengthy letters.

ARTILLERY COMMANDER WITHOUT ARTILLERY

Upon his arrival at Cambridge in July, General Washington took an immediate liking to Knox. A friendship was formed that lasted until Washington's death in 1799. Placed in charge of the Continental Army's artillery, Knox reportedly asked where the artillery was, to which Washington replied there was none.

In the spring of 1775, three weeks after the battles at Lexington and Concord, Ethan Allen and Benedict Arnold had led a successful attack against the British fort at Ticonderoga on Lake Champlain in northern New York. The old fort, built by the French during the French and Indian War, contained a large number of cannons, something the Patriots desperately needed. Arnold made an inventory of the artillery at Ticonderoga and at Crown Point, further north. He began to devise a plan for getting the cannons to Cambridge, the Continental Army's headquarters outside of Boston.

But the cannons never left Ticonderoga. In the fall, aware of the desperate need for artillery, Henry Knox volunteered

An American force commanded by Ethan Allen and Benedict Arnold launched a successful surprise attack on Fort Ticonderoga at dawn on May 10, 1775. In this painting, Allen awakens the commander of Fort Ticonderoga to demand the surrender of the British garrison.

to go to Fort Ticonderoga. Knox was still a civilian volunteer without any rank in the Continental Army. General Washington informed him that "the want of them [cannons] is so great that no trouble or expense must be spared to obtain them." Before leaving Cambridge, Knox wrote to Lucy that "the General has ordered me to go to the Westward as far as Ticonderoga about a three week journey. Don't be afraid, there is no fighting."

Knox's younger brother William went along. The two first traveled to New York City, where Henry Knox surveyed the city's defenses and sent some military supplies back to

Cambridge. They left New York City on November 28, arriving in Albany on December 1 to meet with Major General Philip Schuyler. General Washington had ordered Schuyler, the commander of the Northern Department of the Continental Army, to assist Knox in every way possible. Over the next month, General Schuyler used his influence to ensure that Knox received everything he needed.

Henry Knox arrived at Fort Ticonderoga on December 5, 1775, and began the process of selecting cannons and preparing them for the trip to the northern end of Lake George, about four miles away. In addition to 59 cannons, Knox removed from the stores at Ticonderoga a barrel of flints and 23 hundred-pound boxes of lead for musket balls.

General Philip Schuyler was in charge of the Northern Department of the Continental Army from 1775 to 1777. Washington ordered Schuyler to help Knox with his mission to move the cannons from Fort Ticonderoga.

Ahead lay a truly daunting task: transporting nearly 60 tons of artillery and military supplies about 300 miles across difficult terrain in the dead of winter.

LAKE CROSSING

Late in the afternoon of December 9, after all the cannons and stores had been hauled from Ticonderoga to the northern end of Lake George and loaded onto boats, Knox set off on the fastest vessel. He wanted to complete the 32-mile trip to the southern end of the lake as soon as possible in order to begin arranging for the land transportation of the guns. Almost immediately, however, problems arose. The barge-like vessel carrying the heaviest guns, called a scow, ran aground on a rock. Meanwhile, Knox and the crew of his boat put ashore about halfway down the lake to spend the night.

The following day, the crew of the scow, under the direction of Knox's brother William, managed to get the vessel dislodged, but soon it ran aground again. In the face of a strong headwind, the crew of Knox's boat rowed for 10 hours but failed to reach the south end of the lake. A brisk headwind blew on December 11

—FAST FACT—

Knox submitted to the Continental Congress the following account of his expenses for his mission to Ticonderoga: "For expenditures in a journey from the camp round Boston to New York, Albany, and Ticonderoga, and from thence, with . . . iron and brass ordnance, 1 barrel of flints, and 23 boxes of lead, back to camp (including expenses of self, brother, and servant), £520.15.8¾." In 2005 U.S. dollars, that would be equivalent to about $86,000.

as well, and after setting out shortly before dawn, the men rowed hard for more than six hours, finally arriving at the southern shore of the lake in the early afternoon. Knox wasted no time in dispatching a messenger to a local Patriot, Captain

—FAST FACT—

In addition to bringing cannons to Boston from Ticonderoga, George Washington specifically asked Henry Knox to bring a barrel of musket flints. The flint found naturally in the Ticonderoga area had a reputation as the best flint available for both muskets and arrowheads.

Charles Palmer. He requested that Palmer assemble 40 large sleds, along with teams of oxen and horses to pull them as far as Albany or Kinderhook, where Knox would arrange for new sled teams to complete the journey to Cambridge. The cannons weighed an average of nearly a ton each, and in the absence of good roads, Knox recognized that the only way to transport them would be on sleds over snow.

But at this point there was no snow. Nor, for that matter, were there any cannons, and for several days an uneasy Knox waited for word about his scow and its cargo. By the 16th the cannons had finally arrived. Full of enthusiasm, Knox wrote to George Washington on December 17, "I have had made forty two exceedingly strong sleds & have provided eighty yoke of oxen to drag them as far as Springfield where I shall get fresh cattle to carry them to camp—the rout will be from here to Kinderhook from whence into Great Barrington Massachusetts Bay & down to Springfield." With an adequate snowfall, Knox informed the commander in chief, "I hope in 16 or 17 days to be able to present your Excellency a noble train of artillery. . . ." That proved overly optimistic. Another 40 days would pass before the cannons arrived in Cambridge.

THE LONG TREK TO CAMBRIDGE

On Christmas, Knox awoke to find his eagerly awaited snowfall. But more than two feet had fallen overnight, and the deep drifts made travel extremely difficult. Slowly, Knox's "Noble Train of Artillery" wound its way down the Hudson River valley past Saratoga to Albany. Then a thaw came, making the ice on the Hudson River too thin for the heavy cannons to cross. On two occasions, cannons fell through the ice, but Knox's men were able to recover them.

South of Albany, near Kinderhook, Knox's sled column turned east toward Massachusetts. The greatest obstacle now was the Berkshire Mountains. The men and oxen strained to pull the heavy artillery pieces up the mountainsides, and then struggled to keep them from plummeting down the other sides.

Once Knox and his men reached Springfield on the east side of the Berk-

This wooden canteen is believed to have been owned by Henry Knox.

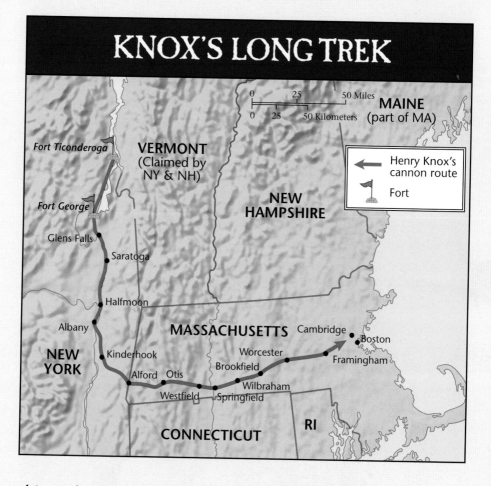

shires, the end of the trek was in sight. With new horses and oxen, the train of artillery finally arrived in Cambridge, Washington's headquarters, in late January. Upon his arrival in Cambridge, Knox learned that Congress had commissioned him a colonel of artillery in the Continental Army.

THE BRITISH ABANDON BOSTON

It was still more than a month before the cannons from Ticonderoga were placed on Dorchester Heights, forcing

This painting depicts Knox's "Noble Train of Artillery," which moved 59 cannons from Fort Ticonderoga to Boston during the winter of 1775–76.

General Howe to abandon Boston. When Howe evacuated the city on March 17, 1776, he took nearly 1,100 Loyalists with him, including Lucy Knox's parents. They settled in Halifax, Nova Scotia, never to return to Boston.

General George Washington rode into Boston at the head of a column of Continental soldiers. Riding at his side was Colonel Henry Knox. The British left 250 large artillery pieces behind, which Knox quickly added to his growing number of cannons for the Continental Army.

While forcing the British out of Boston was cause for jubilation, the city was in terrible shape. Desperate for firewood, the British soldiers and the civilian population had dismantled fences and abandoned buildings to burn for fuel. When Henry Knox went to see what had become of his bookstore, he could find no trace of it. The building and all its contents were gone.

4

THE FIGHT FOR INDEPENDENCE

With the British forced out of Boston, General Washington focused his attention on the defense of New York City. In early April 1776, Washington ordered Henry Knox to move most of the Continental artillery to New York. Only a small number of cannons and soldiers were left in Boston.

On his way to New York, Knox traveled along the coastline, planning coastal defenses in Rhode Island and Connecticut. Lucy Knox accompanied her husband on this journey, and in Fairfield, Connecticut, she gave birth to their first child, Lucy. Throughout the war, Lucy Knox stayed near her husband whenever possible. When circumstances separated them, they devotedly wrote letters back and forth.

ARTILLERY IN THE AMERICAN REVOLUTION

Cannons were the most powerful weapons of the American Revolution, and artillerymen were considered elite troops. It was very difficult for soldiers who did not have artillery support to defeat infantry armed with cannons.

The range of a cannon varied, depending on its size and on the type of shot fired. A cannon might be able to fire an iron ball 800 to 1,200 yards. These cannonballs were good for knocking down walls or damaging fortifications. However, at closer range (300 to 500 yards) cannons often fired containers filled with dozens of small stones or with balls made of iron or lead. This was known as "grapeshot" or "case shot," and was intended to injure or kill large numbers of charging enemy troops. Shells, or bombs—hollow iron balls filled with gunpowder and fitted with fuses—which were fired from mortars, had the same effect. When fired, the shells were supposed to explode over the target, propelling pieces of iron shrapnel into enemy soldiers spread over a wide area.

The cannons used during the 18th century were loaded by pushing the projectile into the muzzle along with a powder charge. Cannons were known by the weight of the projectile; thus, a "six-pound gun" fired an iron cannonball that weighed six pounds. Most of the cannons used in land battles of the Revolution were three-, four-, six-, or twelve-pounders. Commanders preferred these smaller guns because they were easier to maneuver between battles. Larger guns were mounted in forts and on warships.

In the Continental and British armies, the typical gun crew was eight men. Two of these men were gunners, responsible for measuring and preparing the powder charge that would enable the projectile to reach the desired target. This task involved good mathematical skills. The other six members of the gun crew were in charge of bringing up the ammunition, loading it into the cannon, and turning the weapon toward the target.

An earthen breastwork was built to protect this six-pound cannon (left), which is located at Valley Forge.

These iron cannonballs were recovered from the battlefield at Guilford Courthouse in North Carolina.

DEFENDING NEW YORK

Colonel Henry Knox faced a daunting task when he arrived at New York. The British navy was the strongest in the world, while a Continental navy barely existed. The British would own the waters surrounding New York City: New York Harbor, the Hudson River, and the East River. Knox had a limited number of cannons and miles and miles of shoreline to defend.

Knox supervised the construction of **batteries** and fortifications all along the Manhattan waterfront as well as on Brooklyn Heights. He reported to General Washington that he had 121 cannons, but only 520 men who knew how to use them—less than half the number he required. Like the Continental Army as a whole, Knox constantly found himself short of men.

For three months, Knox toiled to make the best of his limited resources. It wasn't until mid-summer 1776 that General William Howe arrived in New York Harbor with an army of more than 32,000 men. For days, Knox watched as more and more British ships appeared on the horizon, sailing into New York Bay to land British troops on Staten Island.

The British fleet, under Admiral Richard Howe, tested the defenses Knox had prepared. Howe sent ships up both the Hudson and East Rivers, drawing fire from the batteries Knox had so carefully placed. The British warships hugged the far shore, at the outer range of Knox's cannons, and were able to sail past the batteries without sustaining significant damage.

CONTINENTAL ARMY ON THE RUN

In late August, General William Howe finally acted, launching an attack against the American positions on Long Island. He nearly captured most of Washington's army. But during the night of August 29, under cover of darkness and fog, more than 9,000 Continental soldiers were evacuated from Brooklyn to Manhattan in small boats.

The amazing maneuver saved Washington's army, but in mid-September General Howe again pressed the attack. This time Howe landed his men at Kip's Bay on the east side of Manhattan. As the British headed west across the island,

Continental soldiers work through the night to move a cannon during the retreat from Long Island.

a large number of Continentals, including Henry Knox, raced north, hoping to avoid being cut off by the British. The Continentals and Knox avoided capture, but they lost cannons and many important supplies. Knox also lost his baggage, leaving him with only the clothes on his back.

The British landing on Manhattan had led to widespread panic among the Continental troops. But General Washington was finally able to re-form his men in northern Manhattan near Harlem Heights.

The failures on Long Island and Manhattan led many to start questioning Washington's abilities as a commander. Was he the right man for the job? During this difficult time, Henry Knox remained staunchly loyal to Washington—as he would throughout the Revolution—calling the commander in chief a good man who could not be everywhere. In Knox's opinion, Washington's officers had let him down.

For his part, Knox continued trying to improve the training and skills of his artillery officers and men. He still faced a shortage of supplies, equipment, and men, even though artillery officers and enlisted men made more money than their counterparts in the infantry.

By early November, the Continental Army had abandoned Manhattan Island to the British except for the area around Fort Washington, a stronghold overlooking the eastern bank of the Hudson River. Nearly 3,000 Americans

Buildings burn while British soldiers beat New Yorkers in this French engraving from 1778. The fire depicted here destroyed about a quarter of New York. It broke out shortly after the British occupied the city in September 1776 and may have been set deliberately by Patriots.

defended the fort and a series of outer fortifications. In command was Knox's good friend General Nathanael Greene, who believed Fort Washington impregnable. On November 16, however, a large force of British soldiers and **Hessians** converged on the American positions. Surrounded, outnumbered, and under the heavy guns of British warships, the Continental garrison surrendered after a few hours of fighting. Greene, who was not at Fort Washington when the assault took place, informed Knox of the disaster in a letter written the following day. "This is a most terrible Event," he told his friend. "Its consequences are justly to be dreaded."

That gloomy assessment was justified. In addition to costing the Continental Army more than 2,800 difficult-to-replace soldiers, Greene's error had opened up all of New Jersey to attack by the British.

WASHINGTON'S MIRACLE

By mid-December, Washington's army had been forced to withdraw all the way across New Jersey to the Pennsylvania side of the Delaware River. Since the British evacuation of Boston in March, the American army had suffered one disaster after another. Morale in the ranks was very low. With many enlistments expiring at the end of December, General Washington needed a miracle to prevent his entire army from disappearing. He planned a risky nighttime maneuver.

On the night of December 25, Washington's entire force would cross the Delaware River and march to Trenton, New Jersey, for a dawn attack on the large contingent of Hessian soldiers who held the town. Washington placed Henry Knox in charge of the embarkation of the men and guns. Under any circumstances, ferrying 2,500 men and 18 artillery pieces across the Delaware at night would have been a difficult undertaking. But as Knox wrote to Lucy, "floating ice in the River made the labour almost incredible." Bitter cold, sleet, and snow added to the Continentals' misery, and it took 10 hours—nearly twice as long as anticipated—before the entire force had landed in New Jersey.

After a difficult march of eight miles, the Continental Army arrived at Trenton around eight o'clock on the morning of the 26th and commenced the attack. Knox noted the "hurry, fright & confusion of the enemy," especially when the Hessians attempted to form in the streets. He had carefully positioned his cannons, which, he wrote to Lucy, "in the twinkling of an eye cleared the streets." The fighting was very one-sided: more than 100 Hessians were killed or wounded before the remaining 900 surrendered, while American casualties totaled only four wounded.

This idealized engraving shows Washington leading his men at the Battle of Trenton, December 26, 1776. Knox was in charge of the dangerous crossing of the Delaware River, and the Americans used 18 of his cannons to capture the Hessian garrison. For his role in the important victory, Knox was promoted to general.

A PROMOTION AND SOME NEW RESPONSIBILITIES

Following the battle, Washington publicly expressed his gratitude to Henry Knox and his artillery for their contribution to the stunning American victory. "The General," Knox revealed in a letter to his brother William, "has done me the unmerited great honor of thanking me in public orders in terms strongly polite." Soon after the Battle of Trenton, Knox received a promotion to brigadier general.

With the Battle of Trenton, and another American victory at Princeton a week later, the British abandoned much of New Jersey. Washington established his winter quarters at Morristown. But while the Continental Army settled in for the winter, General Knox was sent back home to New England. Chief among his tasks was the creation of a laboratory for the manufacture of gunpowder. Springfield, Massachusetts, became the home of this laboratory, and it also served as a government *arsenal*. While in Boston, still mindful of the shortage of men, Knox urged the Massachusetts legislature to increase its efforts to recruit more soldiers for the Continental Army.

It was in Boston that Henry and Lucy Knox were reunited for the first time since the Battle of Long Island in August 1776. But duty called and Knox soon departed. On his way back to Washington's headquarters at Morristown, he stopped along the shores of the Hudson River north of

New York City. There he laid out new defenses in an effort to prevent the British from pushing northward into the strategic Hudson River valley.

THE FIGHT FOR PHILADELPHIA

The year 1777 turned out to be another difficult time for the Continental Army. General William Howe sailed a large force of redcoats and Hessians south from New York City to the Chesapeake Bay. Landing at Head of Elk, Maryland, the force began marching northeast to attack the American capital of Philadelphia. Washington attempted to block Howe's army at Brandywine Creek, southwest of Philadelphia.

When the armies met on September 11, 1777, the British won a clear victory, forcing the Americans to retreat after an afternoon of bloody fighting. Knox's artillerymen had acted "with their usual coolness and intrepidity," as Knox said in a letter to Lucy. Nevertheless, they lost about a dozen artillery pieces when the British infantry overran their positions. With the British victory at Brandywine, the way was open for Howe to take Philadelphia. Redcoats marched unopposed into the rebel capital on September 26. British armies now held the two largest cities in the United States, Philadelphia and New York.

But Washington hoped to dislodge the British from Philadelphia. In the predawn hours of October 4, four columns of American soldiers—about 11,000 men in all—

1776-77 CAMPAIGNS

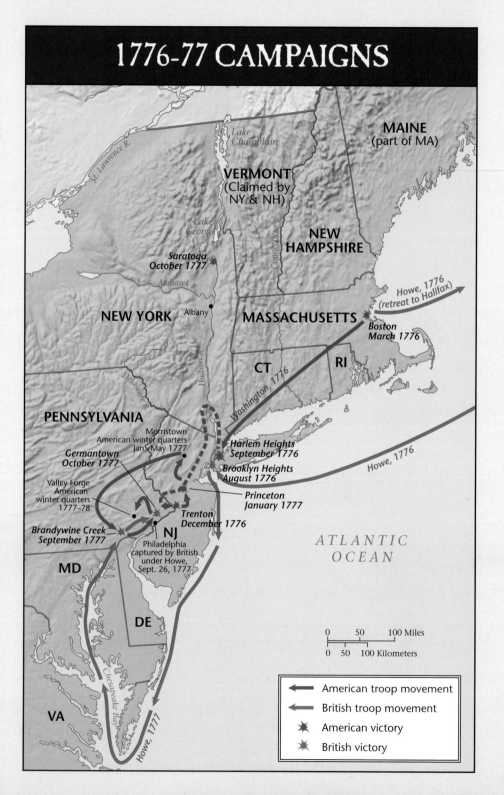

MAINE (part of MA)

Lake Champlain

St. Lawrence R.

VERMONT (Claimed by NY & NH)

Lake George

NEW HAMPSHIRE

Connecticut R.

Saratoga October 1777

Mohawk R.

NEW YORK   Albany

MASSACHUSETTS

Hudson R.

CT

RI

Boston March 1776

Howe, 1776 (retreat to Halifax)

Washington, 1776

PENNSYLVANIA

Morristown
American winter quarters
Jan.–May 1777

Germantown October 1777

Harlem Heights September 1776

Brooklyn Heights August 1776

Howe, 1776

Valley Forge
American
winter quarters
1777–78

Princeton January 1777

Trenton December 1776

Brandywine Creek September 1777

NJ

Philadelphia
captured by British
under Howe,
Sept. 26, 1777

MD

DE

ATLANTIC OCEAN

Delaware R.

0   50   100 Miles
0   50   100 Kilometers

VA

Chesapeake Bay

Howe, 1777

← American troop movement
← British troop movement
✳ American victory
✳ British victory

converged on the village of Germantown, located about five miles north of Philadelphia. There, approximately 9,000 of Howe's soldiers were encamped. The British, caught off guard by the attack, were sent reeling in the initial minutes of the battle. An apparent Continental victory was thwarted, however, when about 120 retreating redcoats took refuge in a large stone mansion owned by Benjamin Chew, the chief justice of Pennsylvania and a staunch Loyalist.

Washington's officers had conflicting advice for the commander in chief regarding what to do about the redcoats barricaded inside the Chew House. Most officers urged Washington simply to bypass the house. After all, the British were retreating in disorder, and it was important that the Continentals press their advantage quickly. But a few officers, including Henry Knox, warned Washington not to leave an entrenched enemy behind his troops. Washington took Knox's advice.

—FAST FACT—

At Harlem Heights in late September 1776, Colonel Henry Knox first proposed the need for a military academy to train professional officers in the art of military science and engineering. In a document titled "Hints for improvement of the Artillery of the United States," Knox wrote that "an Academy established on a liberal plan would be of the utmost service to America." Twenty-six years later, in 1802, the United States Military Academy was established at West Point, New York.

Unfortunately, removing the redcoats from the Chew House proved to be an impossible task. Knox's artillery was brought up, and precious time was lost as round after round

Continental soldiers make a futile attempt to break down the door of the Chew House. Neither repeated infantry assaults nor Knox's artillery could dislodge the redcoats from the house, and American forces lost the initiative at the Battle of Germantown.

bounced off the house's thick stone walls. In the meantime, the British managed to regroup elsewhere in Germantown, and the American advance was stopped. Washington's army retreated, and the Battle of Germantown became another British victory.

Washington didn't blame his artillery commander for the defeat. However, it was one of the rare instances during the war when Knox's advice proved to be wrong.

WINTER AT VALLEY FORGE

Several weeks after the Battle of Germantown, a welcome bit of good news arrived at the American camp in

Whitemarsh, Pennsylvania. During the summer and into the fall of 1777, the British general John Burgoyne had led a large force of redcoats, Hessians, Canadians, and Indians south from Canada through Lake Champlain and into the Hudson Valley. After some initial successes, Burgoyne's campaign bogged down, and he was eventually defeated by an American force under the command of General Horatio Gates. On October 17, the British general surrendered his army to Gates at Saratoga.

For critics in Congress and the army, Saratoga provided another opportunity to question Washington's abilities. Perhaps, they said, someone who actually won battles—like Horatio Gates—would make a better commander in chief of the Continental Army. Despite the calls for Washington to be replaced, Henry Knox's support for his commander remained unwavering.

Washington's army settled in for a miserable winter at Valley Forge, but Henry Knox received a leave of absence to spend time with his beloved Lucy in Boston. While in Boston, Knox continued to lobby for more men and supplies for the Continental Army. As conditions worsened at Valley Forge, however, General Washington ordered Knox to return. The army was hungry, the horses needed to pull the artillery were dying, and the morale of the troops had plummeted. Knox left Boston, but this time he took Lucy with him. Arriving at Valley Forge, she found that the wives of other American generals, including Martha Washington and Caty Greene, had already joined their husbands there.

Good news arrived at General Washington's headquarters in the spring of 1778. The French government had recognized the independence of the United States and had agreed to an alliance. The troops at Valley Forge celebrated, and Knox ordered the firing of a 13-gun salute.

THE REVOLUTION DRAGS ON

Concerned that a French fleet might trap them in Philadelphia, the British decided to abandon the city. In June 1778,

American artillerymen fire their cannons during the Battle of Monmouth, June 28, 1778. The bloody but inconclusive battle, fought on a blisteringly hot day, was the last major engagement in the North. After Monmouth, fighting in the Revolution shifted to the southern colonies.

the redcoats and their Hessian allies began a long trek that would take them across New Jersey and back to New York City.

With the miseries of the winter at Valley Forge behind them, Washington and his generals thirsted for an opportunity to strike at the enemy. That opportunity came on June 28, near Monmouth Court House, New Jersey. When Continental soldiers attacked units guarding the rear of the column, the British army stopped, turned, and launched a massive counterattack. A daylong battle erupted, with the Continental Army holding its own in desperate and savage fighting. At the end of the day, the British withdrew, leaving the field to Washington and his reenergized army.

After the Battle of Monmouth, Henry Knox and his artillery were again warmly praised. "The Corps of Artillery have their full proportion of the Glory of the day," Knox wrote to his brother William after the battle. "His Excellency the General has done them & me the honor to notice us in General orders in very pointed & flattering terms. Indeed I was highly delighted with their coolness, bravery, and good conduct."

With the main British army back in New York City, Henry Knox spent much of the next three years helping to fortify American positions on the Hudson River north of the city. After the Battle of Monmouth, the major battles of the war happened in the South. It was during this period, in

This drawing, made from notes taken by Alexander Hamilton, shows the execution of Major John André. Knox and other Americans admired the British officer and regretted that he had to be hanged as a spy for his part in Benedict Arnold's plot to turn over the fort at West Point to the British.

April 1779, that Congress finally repaid Knox for his expenses in moving the cannons from Ticonderoga to Cambridge more than three years earlier.

In 1780, General Benedict Arnold's plot to turn over West Point to the British was discovered. A Continental patrol captured Major John André, adjutant general in the British army, with plans for the fortifications at West Point. André was tried as a spy. Henry Knox sat as a member of the court-martial board that sentenced André to be hanged.

VICTORY AT YORKTOWN

In the late summer of 1781, General Washington saw an opportunity to deliver the British a crushing blow. After three years of stalemate at New York City, Washington moved his army south to Virginia. Working in conjunction with the French army under General Rochambeau and the French navy, Washington hoped to trap the British commander, Charles Cornwallis, at Yorktown.

Knox undertook the difficult task of moving his artillery from the American positions north of New York City all the

Knox's artillery played an essential role in the siege of Yorktown, Virginia, the last major engagement of the American Revolution. In this painting, the British army of General Charles Cornwallis surrenders at Yorktown, on October 19, 1781.

way to Virginia's Yorktown peninsula. Washington said of Knox's accomplishment that "the resources of his Genius have supplied . . . the defect of means."

The Battle of Yorktown was really a *siege*. By the end of September, French and American armies had Cornwallis hemmed in on the peninsula, with his back to the York River. Meanwhile, a French fleet controlled the surrounding waters. The British were trapped. On October 6, Continental soldiers began digging trenches and erecting earthworks. Three days later, with artillery emplacements in the trenches completed, Knox's big guns rang out, sending cannonballs crashing into Yorktown. Over the ensuing days, a relentless barrage pounded the British positions.

Finally, on October 19, 1781, Lord Cornwallis surrendered. An excited Henry Knox wrote a letter to Lucy, a guest of Mrs. Washington's at Mount Vernon, with news of "a glorious moment for America! This day Lord Cornwallis & his army marches out and piles their arms in the face of our victorious army."

WAR'S END

Despite the victory at Yorktown, the war would continue another two years, with the British still holding onto New York City and the Continental Army in strong positions in the Hudson River Highlands. About a month after Cornwallis's surrender, Knox was promoted to major general. He commanded at West Point in March 1783, when news arrived that a preliminary peace had been signed.

While at West Point in May 1783, Knox organized the Society of the Cincinnati, a group made up of officers in the Continental Army. Washington became the society's first president, and Knox was its first secretary. Knox intended the society as a way for officers to keep in touch after the war, but it generated some controversy that he did not expect. Membership in the society passed down through the eldest son, which to some revolutionaries resembled a new nobility.

When news arrived that the Treaty of Paris, officially ending the war, had been signed in Paris in September 1783,

George Washington embraces Henry Knox during a farewell dinner with his officers at Fraunces Tavern in New York, December 4, 1783.

Henry Knox began negotiations for the British withdrawal from New York City. In early December, shortly after the British pulled out, General Washington met with his officers for a farewell dinner at Fraunces Tavern in New York City. "With a heart full of love and gratitude, I now take leave of you," Washington told his comrades. "I most devoutly wish that your later days may be as prosperous and happy as your former ones have been glorious and honorable." Before he departed, Washington wished to shake the hand of each of his officers one last time. Knox approached first, and the two men embraced warmly. A witness recalled that many of the soldiers broke down and wept.

Henry Knox had given eight years of his life to the cause of independence. He had seen action at Boston and at Brandywine, at Trenton and at Princeton, at Germantown, Monmouth, and Yorktown. Now he wanted to go home. In January 1784, he resigned his commission and returned to Boston to be with Lucy.

5

A NEW NATION

When Henry Knox arrived back in Boston in January 1784, he was 33 years old and eager to return to civilian life with Lucy and his family. In little more than a year, however, Knox would be called back to the service of his country.

SECRETARY AT WAR

On March 8, 1785, the Congress of the United States elected Henry Knox as secretary at war. At the age of 34, Knox found himself in charge of his country's defense. Besides Knox, one clerk and one secretary composed the entire War Department. It was a big task, and Knox frequently wrote to his friend George Washington for advice.

A portrait of Henry Knox, painted in 1784. After the Revolution ended, the general continued to serve his country by taking a government position as secretary at war.

Knox moved to New York City, then the capital of the United States, in April 1785. Lucy and their children followed in the summer. The move to New York put the Knoxes in the middle of the social scene in the federal capital. They hosted dinner parties, and in an acknowledgment of their size, became known as "the greatest couple in New York." While Knox's salary as secretary at war was substantial, he and Lucy spent even more entertaining friends. Knox borrowed money and sold land to help pay his debts, but he would endure financial difficulties for the rest of his life.

As Knox settled in to his new job in New York, word came that his good friend General Nathanael Greene had

Henry Knox's medal from the Society of the Cincinnati, which was formed by American and French officers who had served together during the Revolution. The purpose of the society was to maintain friendships among the officers and their descendants. Knox is wearing this medal in the portrait on p. 54.

died in Georgia in June. Knox's friendship with Greene dated back to the days before the Revolution when he was a frequent visitor to Knox's London Book-Store. Henry and Lucy Knox continued their friendship with Greene's widow, Caty, through the rest of their lives, and even helped provide for the education of Caty's children.

SHAYS'S REBELLION

The United States government had incurred a large debt fighting the Revolutionary War. After peace was declared in 1783, the Congress expected each state to help pay off that debt. In Massachusetts, the heavy taxes imposed by the state government to pay off the national debt caused some farmers to lose their farms, especially in the western part of the state. A revolt, known as Shays's Rebellion, rose up in western Massachusetts. Led by Captain Daniel Shays, the rebellion closed the courts and threatened the safety of the United States Arsenal in Springfield.

Henry Knox was concerned that the 7,000 muskets and 1,300 barrels of powder stored at the arsenal might fall into the hands of Shays's rebels. Knox had established the arsenal during the winter of 1776. Now, as secretary at war, he was responsible for ensuring its safety.

Shays's Rebellion began in August 1786. By January 1787, Knox appointed his wartime friend General Benjamin Lincoln to deal with Shays and his followers. Knowing that

Disgruntled farmers capture a courthouse in Massachusetts, August 1786. The uprising known as Shays's Rebellion showed the weakness of the Articles of Confederation government. The United States had no standing army to speak of, and Knox had great difficulty raising an army to meet the threat.

General Lincoln would soon arrive to protect the Springfield Arsenal, Shays attacked the arsenal on January 25. Shays was defeated, and by mid-February, most of his followers had been captured.

A NEW CONSTITUTION

Shays's Rebellion demonstrated that the U.S. government under the *Articles of Confederation* was inadequate to deal with national emergencies. The rebellion came at a time when many believed there was a need for a more powerful federal government. In January 1787, while dealing with the rebellion in Massachusetts, Knox was one of several friends who replied to a request from George Washington for their thoughts on a stronger government. Plans were soon in place for the meeting of a Constitutional Convention to create a new government for the young United States.

The Constitutional Convention was held in Philadelphia from May to September 1787. George Washington served as president of the convention. After much debate and deliberation, the delegates produced a new constitution, which required the approval of nine states before it went into effect. It wasn't until late 1788 that the first elections were held

—**FAST FACT**—

When Henry Knox served as secretary of war during President Washington's administration, he was one of three employees in the War Department. Today, the United States Department of Defense employs nearly 3 million people.

George Washington presides over the Constitutional Convention, 1787. Washington would later be elected the first president under the new Constitution, and he would bring Knox into his administration as secretary of war.

under the U.S. Constitution. The new government began on April 30, 1789, when George Washington took the oath as the first president of the United States.

IN THE CABINET OF PRESIDENT WASHINGTON

Henry Knox was closely involved in preparations for the inauguration of the president, helping to plan the ceremony and parades. He even had the suit made that Washington wore for his inauguration. After an exhausting day, with all the fanfare surrounding his inauguration, President Washington retired to Henry and Lucy Knox's house in New York

—FAST FACT—

City to watch the fireworks set off in his honor.

Henry Knox was the only cabinet member carried over from the old Confederation government by Washington, a sign of the president's confidence in his old friend. Knox was appointed secretary of war by Washington on September 12, 1789 (since 1785, Knox's title had been secretary *at* war).

In the summer of 1790, the capital of the United States moved from New York to Philadelphia. The federal government had already agreed that a new capital city would be built on the Potomac River between Maryland and Virginia. Philadelphia would be the capital until the new city was ready. The Knoxes moved to Philadelphia along with the federal government.

TROUBLES ON THE WESTERN FRONTIER

From his first years as secretary at war under the Confederation government, troubles with the Indians in the western territories had demanded Knox's attention. Although the treaty that ended the American Revolution called for the British to withdraw from all the forts as far as the Mississippi River,

British troops remained at Fort Niagara and Fort Detroit. The United States suspected that the British were using these posts to stir up the Indians and were providing them with weapons and supplies.

In February 1786, Knox told Congress of his concerns. Just two years earlier, Congress had reduced the number of soldiers in the army to fewer than 100 men. The legislators believed that, with the Revolutionary War over, there was no need for a large standing army. Congress had difficulty raising the money to supply and pay an army.

By 1790, however, difficulties with the Miami and Wabash tribes in the Northwest Territory (today's Ohio, Indiana, Illinois, Michigan, Wisconsin, and parts of Minnesota) led President Washington to send an army to deal with the Indians. The Miami and Wabash had been attacking boat traffic on the Ohio and Wabash Rivers, as well as striking settlements in Kentucky south of the Ohio. President Washington, Henry Knox, and Arthur St. Clair, governor of the Northwest Territory, agreed that a campaign against the Indians was necessary.

Troops under General Josiah Harmar assembled along the Ohio River at Fort Washington (now Cincinnati). Knox believed that Harmar, who had been stationed in the territory since the end of the American Revolution, was best qualified to deal with the Indians. But Harmar was soundly defeated by the Indians, and in March 1791, Washington re-commissioned Arthur St. Clair as a major general to replace him.

St. Clair, with a force of more than 2,000 regular troops and militia, moved from Fort Washington to Miami Village (near today's Fort Wayne, Indiana). St. Clair's force attacked the Miami Indians on November 4, 1791, and was crushed, with hundreds of men killed. Though a congressional commission investigated the disaster and judged St. Clair blameless, he resigned in 1792. Knox would continue to deal with Indian problems in the Northwest Territory for two more years.

SECOND TERM

In 1792, President Washington was reelected. He was sworn in for his second term at Philadelphia on March 4, 1793. Though he longed to return to Massachusetts and the quiet of civilian life, Knox agreed to continue as Washington's secretary of war.

The federal government had no Department of the Navy until 1798. This meant that Knox, as secretary of war, was in charge of both the army and the navy of the United States. In late 1793, Knox introduced a bill to Congress for the construction of six naval *frigates*. His plan was adopted in 1794, and the *Constitution* was the first frigate built. This famous ship, nicknamed "Old Ironsides" when a cannonball bounced of the side of the ship in battle, is still a commis-

Secretary of War Knox asked Congress to pay for six warships. In 1797, the first of these ships, the famed U.S.S. *Constitution*, was launched. The ship, which had a distinguished record in battle, remains a commissioned U.S. Navy warship. This photo of the *Constitution* sailing into Boston Harbor was taken in 1997.

sioned vessel in the United States Navy and can be seen in Charlestown, Massachusetts, not far from where Henry Knox was born in 1750.

Henry and Lucy Knox had not had a home of their own since they fled Boston in the spring of 1775. After the war, they had rented houses in Dorchester and Boston, then in New York City and Philadelphia as Knox's duties took him to the federal capital. Knox desired a home of his own and, while living and working in Philadelphia, decided to have a new home built in Maine. The new home, really a mansion, would stand on land Knox owned along the St. Georges River in Thomaston.

THE WHISKEY REBELLION

The year 1794 proved to be a difficult one for the United States, and much of the burden fell on Henry Knox and the War Department. While still dealing with Indian problems in the Northwest Territory, the United States also had a rebellion in western Pennsylvania to address. The Whiskey Rebellion, which lasted from July to November 1794, was sparked by an *excise tax* on whiskey that the federal government had imposed. In the days before canals, railroads, or even decent roads, western farmers often used their surplus grain to make whiskey, which was easier to ship to eastern markets than whole grains or corn. These farmers believed that the excise tax was an unfair burden on them.

On August 7, 1794, President Washington issued a proclamation and called out the militia to put down the rebellion. Two days later, Henry Knox requested a six-week leave of absence to attend to urgent financial business at home. The president reluctantly gave Knox permission to go home. Knox left Alexander Hamilton, secretary of the Treasury (and a veteran of the Revolution), in charge of the government's response to the Whiskey Rebellion.

It was the only time in nearly 20 years of military and government service that Knox left his post to attend to private affairs. His owed a lot of money, including back taxes on large tracts of land he owned in northern New York and in Maine. During his time in Boston, he did pay more than $400 in taxes on land in Maine. He also, for the first time, visited the site of his new home in Maine, which was under construction.

Knox returned to Philadelphia after eight weeks. By then, the Whiskey Rebellion had been crushed, and the U.S. Army, under General Anthony Wayne, had defeated the Indians in the Northwest Territory.

Wayne, another colleague from the American Revolution, had replaced St. Clair as the head of the troops in the

After several defeats in the Northwest Territory, Knox placed his former colleague General Anthony Wayne in charge of the American forces. Wayne won a decisive victory at the Battle of Fallen Timbers in 1794.

Northwest in 1792. The violence had increased during the summer of 1794, with the Indians attacking Fort Recovery. That attack failed, giving Wayne the advantage. He decisively defeated the Indians at the Battle of Fallen Timbers in northwest Ohio on August 20, 1794. News of the victory arrived in Philadelphia as the federal government dealt with the Whiskey Rebellion.

By December 1794, Henry Knox had been in the service of his country for nearly 20 years, first as a soldier and then as secretary of war. Still only 44 years of age, he was ready to retire from public service and establish a new home for himself and Lucy in Maine. On December 28, 1794, Knox submitted his resignation to President Washington, effective at the end of the year.

6

TWILIGHT AND ACCOMPLISHMENTS

T hough Henry Knox resigned as secretary of war at the end of 1794, he and Lucy didn't leave Philadelphia until June 1795. They arrived at their new home in Thomaston, Maine, on June 22, accompanied by their six surviving children. Half of their 12 children had died of various diseases over the years, and more tragedy was to come.

HOME AND BUSINESS

Knox named his new home Montpelier, in honor of France's help during the Revolution. Knox had come to own several million acres of land in Maine. The land on which Montpelier stood originally belonged to Lucy's grandfather,

This photograph shows a replica of Montpelier, the Knox home in Maine. The original mansion was knocked down in 1871; this building was constructed during the 1930s and today is home to the General Henry Knox Museum.

Brigadier General Samuel Waldo, a veteran of the old French and Indian wars. General Waldo had been the second in command when troops from New England had captured the French stronghold of Louisbourg back in 1745. The property had passed to Lucy's father, Thomas Flucker, and became Lucy's when her parents, loyal to the king, fled Boston in 1775. Henry Knox added to the land by purchasing more than 3 million acres while he was secretary of war.

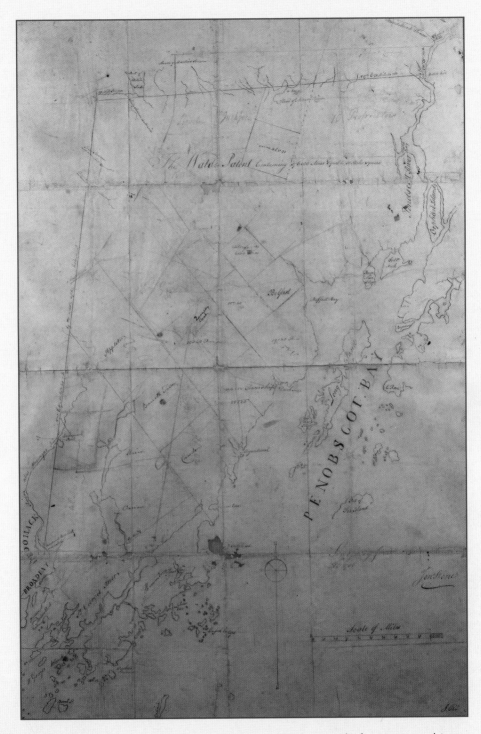

A map of General Samuel Waldo's property in Maine, made for Henry and Lucy Knox in 1786.

Shortly after their arrival at Montpelier, the Knoxes celebrated the Fourth of July by hosting a party for 500 people. Soon Knox plunged into various business opportunities to generate money from his land, including brick-making, lime-burning, farming, lumbering, fishing, shipbuilding, and even an attempt at canal building. Nevertheless, he continued to struggle financially; he would probably have been better off concentrating on one or two endeavors. In the evenings, he and Lucy enjoyed playing chess, with Lucy reportedly the better player.

Over the next three years, Lucy and Henry Knox suffered the loss of three more children to disease, including two who died on the same day. Only three of their children were destined to outlive their parents.

Though retired, Knox took part in official ceremonies. He attended the launching of the navy frigate *Constitution* in Boston in September 1797, six years after he, as secretary of war, had suggested its construction. In 1801, the citizens of his district elected Knox to the Massachusetts legislature, and in 1802 the governor appointed Knox a justice of the peace for Lincoln County.

UNTIMELY DEATH

On October 25, 1806, Henry Knox died at the age of 56. His son Henry J. Knox reported that his father had swallowed a chicken bone, which had become lodged in his intestine. Knox was buried under his favorite oak tree near Montpelier with full military honors.

Knox's reputation as an officer who could get things done, and as an administrator who could cope with adversity, endures to this day. Each March 17, Bostonians celebrate Evacuation Day, commemorating the British withdrawal from their city in 1776. That early triumph of the Revolution was made possible only by Knox's remarkable feat in moving cannons from Fort Ticonderoga to Cambridge. During that long-ago winter, one 25-year-old Patriot simply would not give up until he had completed his Herculean task.

Artifacts from Montpelier: (right) a mahogany wardrobe made for General Knox about 1790; (below) a porcelain chocolate pot and matching mugs, made in Guangzhou, China, for Knox about 1790. The delicate china is decorated with the emblem of the Society of the Cincinnati and marked with the initials HLK.

Chronology

1750: Henry Knox is born on July 25 in Boston, the 7th of 10 sons of William Knox and Mary Campbell.

1759: At the age of nine, Henry Knox begins working at a bookstore.

1770: The Boston Massacre happens on March 5, with British guards opening fire at the Customs House after a mob pelted them with snow, ice, and stones.

1771: Henry Knox opens his London Book-Store in Boston.

1773: On December 16, colonists protest the tax on tea by dumping tea from ships into Boston Harbor, an event that becomes known as the Boston Tea Party.

1774: The British close the Port of Boston on June 1 in response to the Boston Tea Party. Henry Knox marries Lucy Flucker on June 16.

1775: The Battles of Lexington and Concord, on April 19, mark the beginning of the American Revolution.

1776: On March 5, Americans place cannons on Dorchester Heights, leading to the British evacuation of Boston on March 17. Knox commands the artillery during the American losses on Long Island and on Manhattan. Knox plays a critical role in the defeat of the Hessians at the Battle of Trenton on December 26.

1777: Knox again plays a role in the Battle of Princeton in January. He establishes the arsenal at Springfield, Massachusetts, during the winter, and is present at the battles of Brandywine and Germantown in the fall. While the Continental troops settle in for another hard winter at Valley Forge, Henry Knox, on leave, spends time with Lucy in Boston.

1778: Henry Knox and his artillery receive great praise for their performance at the Battle of Monmouth in June.

1781: The surrender of Lord Cornwallis at Yorktown on October 19 marks the end of major fighting in the Revolutionary War.

1783: Henry Knox organizes the Society of the Cincinnati while at West Point, New York. The Treaty of Paris, ending the war, is signed in September. Knox supervises the formal turnover of occupied New York City to Continental troops in December.

1784: Henry Knox resigns his commission and returns to Boston.

1785: Henry Knox is elected secretary at war in the Confederation government, a post he is to hold for nearly 10 years.

1786: Shays's Rebellion in western Massachusetts, beginning in August, threatens the United States Arsenal there. Knox appoints General Benjamin Lincoln to deal with the rebellion, which is crushed by February 1787.

1787: The Constitutional Convention is held in Philadelphia from May to September; it draws up the new Constitution of the United States.

1789: George Washington is sworn in as the first president of the United States on April 30. Henry Knox is asked to continue as secretary of war under the new government.

1794: Henry Knox copes with the Whiskey Rebellion in western Pennsylvania from July to November. General Anthony Wayne defeats the Indians at the Battle of Fallen Timbers on August 20, ending years of Indian uprisings in the Northwest Territory. Knox resigns as secretary of war at the end of the year.

1801: Henry Knox is elected to the Massachusetts legislature.

1806: Henry Knox dies on October 25 at the age of 56.

Glossary

Articles of Confederation—the document on which the government of the United States was based from 1777 until 1789.

arsenal—a place where arms and military equipment are stored.

artillery—large-diameter guns such as cannons, howitzers, and mortars, which fire either solid cannon balls or exploding shells.

battery—a grouping of artillery pieces.

Continentals—members of the Continental Army, formed in June 1775 by Congress. These were regular troops who enlisted to serve a given period of time during the American Revolution.

excise tax—a tax on the production or sale of certain types of merchandise.

fascines—bundles of saplings and branches bound together with rope or vines and used to construct fortifications and earthworks.

frigate—a fast, square-rigged warship of the 18th and early 19th centuries that carried fewer guns than the largest warships of the day, known as ships of the line.

Hessians—German professional soldiers, or mercenaries, hired by the British to fight in the Revolutionary War.

Loyalist—an American who remained loyal to King George III and the British government during the American Revolution.

militia—civilians called upon during an emergency to fight the enemy. When not needed, militia troops remain at home and carry on their daily lives.

Patriots—those supporting the fight for independence from Great Britain.

rebels—what the British called those fighting against the king during the American Revolution because they were rebelling against the established government.

redcoats—British soldiers.

redoubt—a small fortification, usually including cannons, built of earth and wood as part of a series of fortifications.

siege—a military tactic of surrounding an enemy fort or city and preventing food or reinforcements from reaching the enemy. Often, artillery is used to convince the enemy to surrender or to destroy part of the fort so that troops can attack it.

Further Reading

Books for Students:

Herbert, Janis. *The American Revolution for Kids: A History with 21 Activities*. Chicago: Chicago Review Press, 2002.

Murray, Stuart. *Eyewitness: American Revolution*. New York: Dorling Kindersley Publishing, 2002.

Reit, Seymour. *Guns for General Washington*. New York: Harcourt Brace & Co., 1990. (Historical fiction)

Strum, Richard M. *Causes of the American Revolution*. Stockton, N.J.: OTTN Publishing, 2005.

Books for Older Readers:

Callahan, North. *Henry Knox: General Washington's General*. New York: Rinehart & Co., 1989.

McCullough, David. *1776*. New York: Simon & Schuster, 2005.

Middlekauff, Robert. *The Glorious Cause: The American Revolution, 1763–1789*. 2nd edition. New York: Oxford University Press, 2005.

http://www.fort-ticonderoga.org

The official website of Fort Ticonderoga.

http://www.generalknoxmuseum.org

The official website of Montpelier, the re-created home of General Henry Knox in Thomaston, Maine.

http://www.nps.gov/revwar

This National Park Service website includes links to numerous American Revolutionary War sites. It also features a time line, biographies, and educational resources related to America's War of Independence.

http://www.southbostoncitizens.org/sbca_history.htm

The official website of the South Boston Citizens' Association, which organizes the annual Evacuation Day activities each year in Boston on the anniversary of the British withdrawal from the city in 1776.

http://www.americaslibrary.gov/cgi-bin/page.cgi/jb/ revolut

This site from the Library of Congress offers information about different events and people from the American Revolution.

Index

Numbers in **bold italics** refer to captions.

Picture Credits

About the Author

RICHARD M. STRUM was born in Ticonderoga, New York. He earned his BA at Houghton College and MAEd at the College of William and Mary. Rich is the Director of Interpretation & Education at Fort Ticonderoga. He is the author of *Ticonderoga: Lake Champlain Steamboat*, a book for adults about the last passenger steamboat on Lake Champlain. He is also the author of two other books for children: *Fort Ticonderoga* and *Causes of the American Revolution*. He lives in Ticonderoga, New York, with his wife Martha and daughters Mackenzie, Kirsten, and Eliza.